It was her range of notes

that caused all the commotion.

With one breath she sounded like rain,

sprinkling high notes in the morning sun.

And with the next she was thunder,

resounding deep in a dark sky.

SEASON OF TWO THOUSAND AND TWO

SCHOLASTIC PRESS · NEW YORK · PRESENTS

When Marian Sang

The True Recital of Marian Anderson

The Voice of a Century

Libretto by . . . . PAM MUÑOZ RYAN

Staging by . . . . BRIAN SELZNICK

No one was surprised

that Marian loved to sing. After all, she listened to Father singing in the morning as he dressed. Mother often hummed while she worked in the kitchen. Sometimes Marian and her little sisters, Ethel May and Alyse, sang songs all afternoon.

Let us break bread together
on our knees
Let us break bread together
on our knees
When I fall on my knees
with my face to the rising sun
O Lord, have mercy on me.

However, *her* voice was distinct — strong and velvety and able to climb more than twenty-four notes.

Everyone wanted to hear Marian sing.

Alexander Robinson, the choir director at the Union Baptist Church in South Philadelphia, wanted to hear Marian sing even though she was not quite eight years old and sometimes sang *too* loud. He asked her to perform a duet with her friend Viola Johnson. As Viola sang the high part and Marian sang the low, their harmony blended like a silk braid.

Dear to the heart of the Shepherd
Dear are the sheep of His fold
Dear is the love that He gives them
Dearer than silver or gold.

Church folks started whispering and followed with out-and-out talking about Marian's remarkable gift.

Neighboring churches heard the news and invited Marian to perform. One advertisement said: "COME AND HEAR THE BABY CONTRALTO, TEN YEARS OLD." And people came.

When Marian sang, it was often with her eyes closed, as if finding the music within. Audiences heard not only words, but feelings too: spirited worship, tender affection, and nothing short of joy.

She was chosen for the celebrated People's Chorus, a hundred voices from all the black church choirs in Philadelphia. She was one of the youngest members and had to stand on a chair so those in the back could see the pride of South Philadelphia.

Her father was proud too, but protective. He didn't want anyone taking advantage of his child. Father's love made Marian feel important. When he died after an injury at the Reading Terminal where he sold ice, tragedy filled Marian's heart and sometimes her songs.

Were you there when they laid Him
in the tomb?
Were you there when they laid Him
in the tomb?
Oh . . . oh . . . sometimes it causes me
to tremble, tremble, tremble
Were you there when they laid Him
in the tomb?

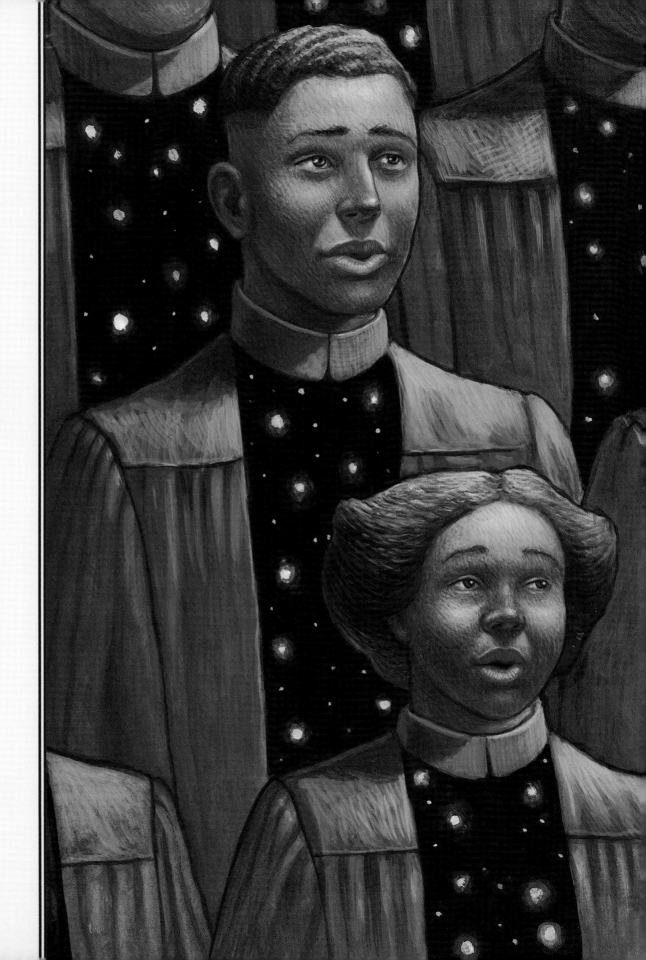

Mother was happy for Marian's success but reminded her that no matter what she studied to take a little extra time and do it well.

Marian didn't need extra encouragement when it came to singing. She practiced her part of each song and often learned all the other parts too. For her, music was serious business, and more than anything, she hoped to someday go to music school. Church members promised tuition for "our Marian" if she was accepted.

Since Father's death, Marian worked at odd jobs and sang in concert programs in order to help support her family. It wasn't until 1915, when Marian was eighteen, that she finally went to a music school and patiently waited in line for an application. But the girl behind the counter helped everyone except Marian. Was she invisible?

Finally, the girl said, "We don't take colored!" Her voice sounded like a steel door clanking shut.

Marian knew about prejudice. She had seen the trolley drive past her family as they stood at the corner. She knew that her people were always the last to be helped in a store. But she could not understand how anyone who was surrounded by the spirit and beauty of music could be so narrow-minded.

She felt sick in her stomach and in her heart. Didn't they know that her skin was different but her feelings were the same? Couldn't she be a professional singer if she was Negro?

With unwavering faith, Mother told her that there would be another way to accomplish what would have been done at that school. Marian believed her mother. She took voice lessons in her own neighborhood, continued with the choirs, and sometimes performed at Negro churches and colleges.

When Marian saw a Metropolitan Opera performance of the tragic opera *Madame Butterfly*, thoughts of a formal music education again came to mind. How wonderful it would be to sing on a grand stage, act out a dramatic role, and wear beautiful costumes. The passionate music inspired her and she was determined to study. But opera was simply the sun and the moon — a dream that seemed too far away to reach.

He's got the wind and the rain
    in His hands
He's got the sun and the moon
    right in His hands
He's got the wind and the rain
    in His hands
He's got the whole world in His hands.

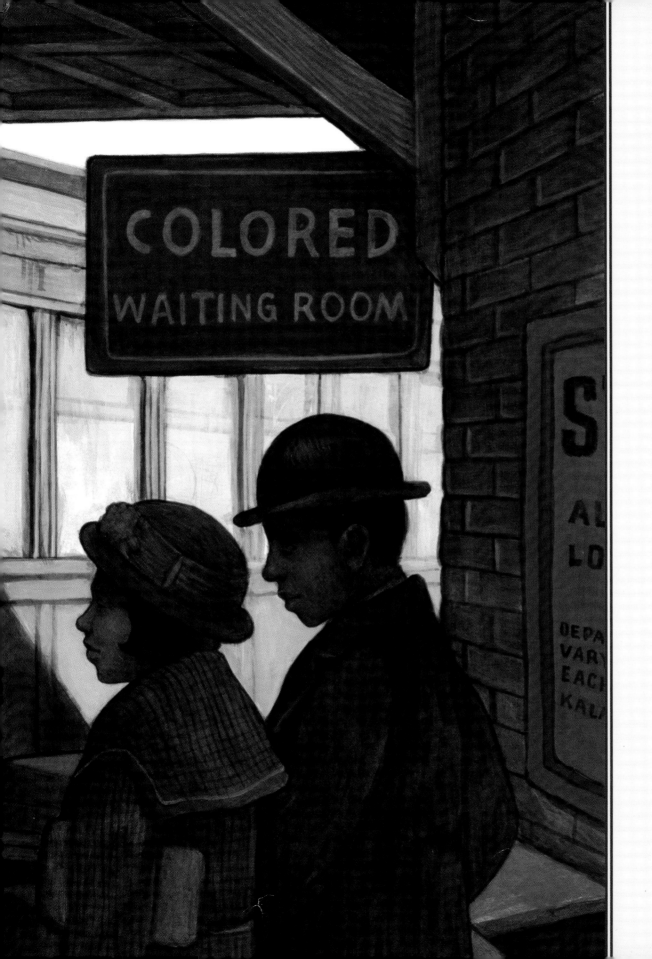

As a young woman in her twenties, Marian was invited to many states to sing. Sometimes she traveled with her accompanist by train where they were seated in the dirty and crowded Jim Crow car reserved for Negroes. When she arrived at her destination, she often sang the same program twice, to separate audiences — one white and one black — or to segregated groups, whites in the best seats and blacks in the balcony. Many times, she was welcomed enthusiastically by her audiences, and then could not get a hotel room because she was Negro.

No matter what humiliations she endured, Marian sang her heart with dignity. Her voice left audiences weeping or in hushed awe as they strained to hold on to the memory of every opulent note.

When Israel was in Egypt's Land

Let my people go

Oppressed so hard they could not stand

Let my people go

Go down Moses

Way down in Egypt's Land

Tell ol' Pharaoh

To let my people go.

Marian still wanted to advance her singing with master teachers. With the help of friends, she was granted an audition with the fierce yet famous Giuseppe Boghetti.

When she arrived at his studio, Mr. Boghetti announced that he didn't have time or room for new students. Too afraid even to look at him, Marian took a deep breath. Slowly, with great emotion, she sang,

> *"Deep river, my home is over Jordan*
> *Deep river, Lord, I want to cross over*
>   *into campground*
> *Don't you want to go to that gospel feast*
> *That promised land where all is peace?*
> *O, deep river, Lord, I want to cross over*
>   *into campground."*

Marian finally lifted her eyes.

"I will make room for you right away," Mr. Boghetti said firmly, "and I will need only two years with you. After that, you will be able to go anywhere and sing for anybody."

Again, Marian's devoted church community raised the money for her lessons.

Marian worked hard with Mr. Boghetti, and sometimes, for practice, she sang scenes from Italian operas with him. Her recitals now included German songs too, but other languages troubled her. She didn't want simply to sing beautiful words like *Dunkel, wie dunkel in Wald und in Feld!* She wanted to know that the words meant *Dark, how dark in the woods and the fields!*

Other Negro singers had gone overseas to develop their voices and learn foreign languages. Why not her? After all, Europe was different. There, she would be able to sing to mixed audiences and travel without the restrictions put on her people in America.

Marian needed to grow and Mother agreed.

A bundle of trepidation and excitement, Marian boarded the *Ile de France* in October 1927. She had never been so far from her family. She knew her sisters would take good care of Mother, but still she already felt twinges of homesickness.

Sometimes I feel like a motherless child

Sometimes I feel like a motherless child

Sometimes I feel like a motherless child

A long ways from home. A long ways from home.

Sometimes I feel like I'm almost gone

Sometimes I feel like I'm almost gone

Sometimes I feel like I'm almost gone

A long ways from home. A long ways from home.

Marian studied and was eventually invited to perform in concert halls in Norway, Sweden, Finland, and Denmark. The enthusiasm for her singing was so overwhelming that one newspaper in Sweden called it "Marian Fever."

Audiences applauded in London, cheered in Paris, and pounded on the stage for encores in Russia. In Austria, the world-famous conductor, Arturo Toscanini, announced that what he had heard, one was privileged to hear only once in a hundred years.

Marian felt as if she had finally achieved some success. She even asked Mother if there was anything she wanted that would make her happy because now Marian could afford to buy it for her. Mother said that all she wanted was for God to hold Marian in the highest of His hands.

It seemed like she was already there.

Mr. Boghetti had been right. She *could* go anywhere and sing for anyone . . .

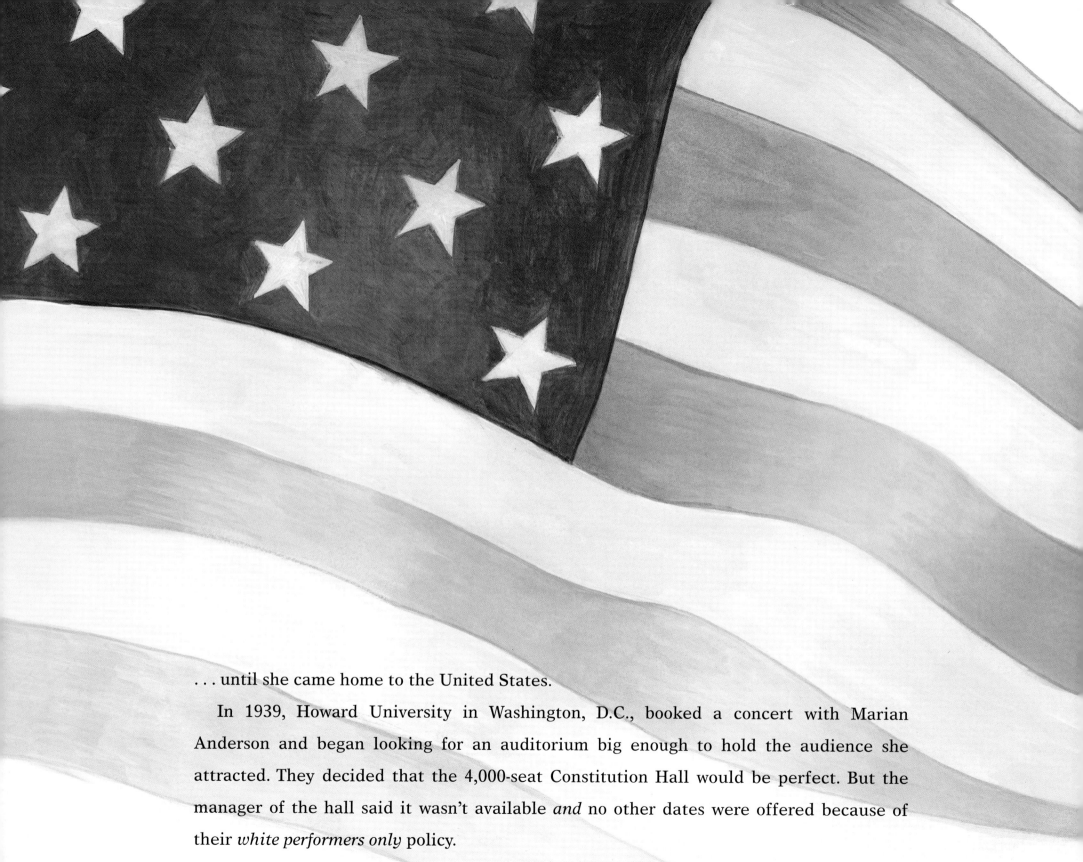

. . . until she came home to the United States.

In 1939, Howard University in Washington, D.C., booked a concert with Marian Anderson and began looking for an auditorium big enough to hold the audience she attracted. They decided that the 4,000-seat Constitution Hall would be perfect. But the manager of the hall said it wasn't available *and* no other dates were offered because of their *white performers only* policy.

Marian's agent, Sol Hurok, wrote to the hall manager, pointing out that Marian Anderson was one of the greatest living singers of our time. But it did no good.

Enraged fans wrote letters to the newspaper. In protest, Eleanor Roosevelt, the first lady of the United States, resigned from the organization that sponsored Constitution Hall.

Howard University then tried to reserve a large high school auditorium from an all-white school. Again, they were denied. Now teachers were angry and marched in support of Marian in front of the Board of Education. Washington, D.C., was a boiling pot about to spill over.

Wasn't there someplace in her own country's capital where Marian Anderson's voice could be heard?

Committees formed and held meetings. Finally, with President Roosevelt's approval, the Department of the Interior of the United States government invited Marian to sing on the steps of the Lincoln Memorial on Easter Sunday. Her country was offering her a momentous invitation, but she had concerns. Would people protest? Was it dangerous? Would anyone come?

Examining her heart, Marian realized that although she was a singer first and foremost, she also had become a symbol to her people and she wanted to make it easier for those who would follow her.

She said yes.

Standing in the shadow of the statue of Lincoln, waiting to be called out, she read the engraved words: . . . THIS NATION UNDER GOD SHALL HAVE A NEW BIRTH OF FREEDOM. . . .

Marian looked out on a river of 75,000 people. Her heart beat wildly. Would she be able to utter one note?

She took a deep breath and felt the power of her audience's goodwill surge toward her. Marian's sisters were there, and Mother too. Marian stood straight and tall. Then she closed her eyes and sang,

"My country 'tis of thee
Sweet land of liberty . . .
Let freedom ring!"

A roaring cheer followed every song. At the end of the program, the people pleaded for more.

When she began her thought-provoking encore,

"Oh, nobody knows the trouble I see
Nobody knows my sorrow...."

. . . silence settled on the multitudes.

For almost sixteen years after the Lincoln Memorial performance, Marian sang for kings and queens, presidents and prime ministers, famous composers and conductors. She received medals, awards, and honorary degrees for her magnificent voice. But there was still one place Marian had not sung. When she was finally invited, a dream came true.

Marian wondered how people would react. No Negro singer had ever done such a thing. She would be the first. But she didn't need to worry. After she signed the contract, someone said, "Welcome home."

On opening night excitement charged the air. As Marian waited in the wings, the orchestra began. Her stomach fluttered. She walked onto the grand stage. Trembling, she straightened her costume and waited for the pounding music she knew to be her cue.

Tonight was her debut with the Metropolitan Opera. At long last, she had reached the sun and the moon.

The curtains parted . . .

. . . and Marian sang.

Encore

"Genius, like justice, is blind. For genius has touched with the tip of her wing this woman. . . . She has endowed Marian Anderson with such voice as lifts any individual above his fellows, as is a matter of exultant pride to any race."

— Secretary of the Interior Harold Ickes at the Lincoln Memorial Concert, 1939

FROM THE AUTHOR • After the publication of *Amelia and Eleanor Go for a Ride*, Brian Selznick and I discussed how that book had prompted so many people to tell us their own Eleanor Roosevelt stories. Brian mentioned that his uncle had confided a story too — one that involved Eleanor Roosevelt, Marian Anderson, and the Lincoln Memorial concert. I was immediately intrigued.

I love spirituals, gospel music, musicals, and opera (when I was in junior high, I sang in an all-city honor chorus). Like many people, I knew a little about Marian Anderson — most specifically about her Lincoln Memorial concert. After Brian's mention, I began researching and became fascinated by the depth of her talent. I felt as if I'd been introduced to someone who was a kindred spirit to other characters about whom I'd written: Charlotte Parkhurst in *Riding Freedom*, Amelia Earhart and Eleanor Roosevelt, and Esperanza in *Esperanza Rising* — all women who overcame society's limitations and whose stories deserved to be told. Marian Anderson was someone for whom all Americans, especially children, could be proud. I wanted more people to know her inspiring story. It was with that passion and conviction that I set out to write this book.

By 1939, when Marian was 42, she had been singing in hundreds of venues in the United States. But it was the Lincoln Memorial concert that attracted the attention of the nation. Constitution Hall in Washington, D.C., run by the Daughters of the American Revolution, had allowed other African Americans to perform there in the past, but there had been issues about seating when black and white patrons attended. The D.A.R.'s solution was to accept only white performers. Even with Secretary of the Interior Harold Ickes' plea to the D.A.R. in support of Marian Anderson, the Board of Management voted 39 to 1 *not* to make an exception for her.

Marian was an uncomfortable activist. Unlike many who formed committees and spoke out against this incident, Marian was hesitant to make statements and preferred to find other ways to respond to the injustice. But this event became symbolic of much that was wrong in our country at that time and even Eleanor Roosevelt took action. She wrote to the D.A.R., ". . . I feel obliged to send in to you my resignation. You had an opportunity to lead in an enlightened way and it seems to me that your organization has failed." On February 27, 1939, in her syndicated "My Day" column, Mrs. Roosevelt announced her resignation.

In her autobiography, *My Lord, What a Morning*, Marian Anderson calls Eleanor Roosevelt "…one of the most admirable human beings I have ever met." Marian and Eleanor became friends and sometimes their paths crossed in unlikely places where Marian was singing and Eleanor was speaking. Once, a stage manager told Marian that Mrs. Roosevelt would be at the same theater a few days later and would occupy the same dressing room. In friendship, Marian left her a welcome message on the mirror, written with a bar of soap.

Marian did not harbor bad feelings against the D.A.R. She always indicated that the group should not be blamed for what she felt was the influence of a few. In 1942, three years after she had been banned, the D.A.R. invited Marian to sing at Constitution Hall on behalf of the war effort. She said yes, but only if the seating was mixed. The D.A.R. agreed to Marian's request! It was the first time in Constitution Hall's history that blacks and whites sat together.

At times Marian was criticized for not taking a stronger stand against segregation. But she felt it was also extremely important to have a black role model to represent accomplishments for her people. As a compromise, she sometimes insisted on vertical seating. This meant an invisible line was drawn down the middle of a concert hall, whites on one side and blacks on the other, so there would be an equal amount of all types of seats for both races. By 1952, influenced by activists and her own conscience, Marian began to insist that she would perform only for mixed audiences. She remained dedicated to making the road easier for other African-American singers and her success *did* pave the way.

Marian Anderson sang in eight languages. She performed three times on the steps of the Lincoln Memorial. First, in 1939; again, in 1952 at the memorial service for Secretary of the Interior Harold Ickes, who had introduced her on that first occasion, and almost 25 years later in 1963 at the March on Washington for Jobs and Freedom with Martin Luther King, Jr. In 1958, she was appointed to the 13th United Nations delegation. She sang at the inaugurations of Presidents Dwight D. Eisenhower and John F. Kennedy and was the recipient of the NAACP's Spingarn Medal, the Kennedy Center Honors, and the Presidential Medal of Freedom, the highest civilian award in America. At her Metropolitan Opera debut, in Verdi's *Un Ballo in Maschera (The Masked Ball)*, she was 57 years old, her voice still rich and abundant.

Marian was married to Orpheus Fisher, a New York architect. They had no children but she was very close to her nephew, James DePriest, a composer and symphony orchestra conductor. Family, faith, and music remained strong threads in her life, especially the influence of her mother's belief in the ultimate goodness of people's hearts.

All her life, Marian sang her soul. Her rendition of "Were You There When They Crucified My Lord?" can make the most callous weep. The angst of an era, the yearning for people to learn and accept, and the unfailing hope for humankind were all there in her voice. And the world heard it when Marian sang.

FROM THE ILLUSTRATOR • My uncle, Richard Selznick, was the family storyteller. While I was working on *Amelia and Eleanor Go for a Ride*, I brought some of my photographic research to my little cousin's house because she was working on a report about Eleanor Roosevelt for school. The photograph shown here, of Eleanor Roosevelt presenting Marian Anderson with the Spingarn Medal, was

among them. When my uncle saw this picture, he said, "I knew both of those women." "You knew Eleanor Roosevelt and Marian Anderson?" I asked incredulously. He told me he remembered being a college student in Washington, D.C., when they were there for Marian Anderson's historic concert, and he helped bring them around town. Wow.

I called Pam Muñoz Ryan to tell her this story, and a few days later she told me she wanted to write a book about Marian Anderson inspired by my uncle's recollection. I was thrilled, and so was my uncle.

The highlight of my research was a trip to the Marian Anderson Historical Society, which is located in Marian Anderson's home in South Philadelphia. Blanche Burton-Lyles is the founder and president of the Society, and as a child, she played piano at parties given by Marian Anderson. Ms. Burton-Lyles became the first female African-American pianist to graduate from the Curtis Institute of Music and went on to have a celebrated career as a concert pianist. She also runs a protégé program, which helps gifted young African-American musicians, and I had the pleasure of meeting one of the protégés, Soprano Lisa Marie. They sat me down in the living room, Blanche took her place at the piano, and standing in front of a portrait of Marian Anderson, Lisa Marie sang "Walk With Me, Jesus," a spiritual that Marian Anderson used to sing. It was deeply moving.

They let me photograph the house, and then they took me on a tour of Marian Anderson's Philadelphia, from what was possibly the music school that rejected her because she was black, to the church she attended, to her birth home. Blanche even showed me old wallpaper she had uncovered that might have been in the Anderson home. I used that pattern in the picture of Marian as a child singing with her family.

Another major source of visual research was the archives at the Metropolitan Opera. Pam and I spent a wonderful day there, along with our editor, Tracy Mack. We went on a backstage tour and spent a few hours in the archives with archivist John Pennino, and in the evening, we saw a revival of the very opera in which Marian Anderson made her debut, *Un Ballo in Maschera*. I returned to the archives several times to continue my research. The old Metropolitan Opera was torn down in the sixties, so I relied on pictures to accurately represent the opera house where Marian sang. The wall of photographs behind Giuseppe Boghetti in this book is based on a similar wall in the Met archives. In the picture of Marian being comforted by her mother, the wallpaper behind them is the pattern of the curtains at the old Metropolitan Opera, a hint of good things to come.

I had originally intended to show Marian singing at the Lincoln Memorial from her point of view, that is, from the stage looking out into the crowd. But I saw a mural at the Department of the Interior in Washington, D.C., that was painted to commemorate Marian's concert ("An Incident in Contemporary American Life," 1942, Mitchell Jamieson), and it showed the concert from the *crowd's* point of view. We are inside the sea of people, black and white together, and in the distance we can just barely see Marian. I was very touched by this mural and used it as the basis of the far left-hand section of my painting.

My uncle died this year, so he won't ever see the finished book. I have since discovered that he was in fact only 12 years old in 1939, the year of Marian Anderson's historic concert, so he could not have actually been there as a college student. Perhaps he met Marian Anderson and Eleanor Roosevelt at one of Marian's return engagements in D.C. We'll never know. My uncle always said that stories often get exaggerated as they are retold. He used the Yiddish word *bubbeh mayse*, which means "grandmother's tale" or "tall tale." But this accidental memory of his led to the very book you are now holding. If you look again at the picture of the crowd listening to Marian Anderson at the Lincoln Memorial, on the left side you can see a round-faced young man wearing glasses, facing you with his eyes closed. That's my uncle. He finally made it to the concert.

Ovations

The author and illustrator applaud the following people and organizations for their direction and assistance:

Blanche Burton-Lyles, founder and president of the Marian Anderson Historical Society, for showing us Marian Anderson's Philadelphia and for her personal recollections; Soprano Lisa Marie, who sang for us in Marian Anderson's home; the National Archives and Records Administration; John Pennino and Robert Tuggle at the New York Metropolitan Opera Company; Mary Louise VanDyke at Oberlin College and the *Dictionary of American Hymnology*; the University of Pennsylvania; and especially Allan Keiler, author of the consummate biography, *Marian Anderson: A Singer's Journey*, for his invaluable expertise.

To find out more about Marian Anderson, read her autobiography, *My Lord, What a Morning*, Viking Press, 1956, reprinted by University of Illinois Press, 2001; and *Marian Anderson: A Singer's Journey*, by Allan Keiler, Scribner, 2000. Young students can also read *Marian Anderson: A Great Singer* (Great African Americans Series) by Patricia C. McKissack, Enslow Publishers, Inc., 1991, revised edition 2001. Watch the video *Marian Anderson: The Story of the Voice that Broke Barriers*, WETA, Washington, D.C., 1991. Visit the University of Pennsylvania Library's virtual exhibition at http://www.library.upenn.edu/special/gallery/anderson, and the Marian Anderson Historical Society at http://www.mariananderson.org.

To view Mrs. Roosevelt's letter of resignation to the president general of the D.A.R. visit http://www.nara.gov/exhall/originals/eleanor.html.

The quotes from this book (excluding song lyrics) come from *My Lord, What a Morning*. In order of their appearance in this text, they can be referenced on the following pages of the autobiography: 14, 29, 38, 49, 148, 301, and 196.

The photograph of Marian Anderson and Eleanor Roosevelt is reprinted courtesy of the Metropolitan Opera Archives.

In order to address the era in which this story took place, the author has, with the greatest respect, stayed true to the references to African Americans as colored or Negro. Marian Anderson referred to herself and others of her race in this manner in the entirety of her autobiography.

Marian Anderson's legacy continues through the Marian Anderson Historical Society, and its protégé program for the advancement and scholarship of aspiring artists, 762 South Marian Anderson Way, Philadelphia, Pennsylvania, 19146-1822.

Notable Dates in Marian Anderson's Life

1897 – Born in Philadelphia on February 27.

ca 1903 – Age 6. Performs with Union Baptist Church Junior Choir.

ca 1907 – Age 10 or 11. Chosen for the People's Chorus.

1909 – Marian's father, John Berkley Anderson, dies at age 34.

1912 – Age 15. Marian postpones entrance to high school to help support her family.

1915 – Age 18. Denied entrance to music school. Enters William Penn High School.

1918 – Age 21. Transfers to South Philadelphia High School.

1920 – Age 23. Auditions for Giuseppe Boghetti.

1921 – Age 24. Graduates from high school.

1924 – Age 27. First African-American concert artist to record spirituals for a major American recording company (Victor). First African-American artist to appear as a soloist with the Philadelphia Philharmonic Society.

1925 – Sings with the New York Philharmonic Society. Receives rave reviews.

1929 – Concert tours in the United States.

1930 – Concert tours in Germany, Scandinavia, and the United States.

1935 – Concert tours in France, the United States, Russia, and Austria. Sings at Salzburg Festival, where Arturo Toscanini is present.

1936 – Sings at Carnegie Hall in New York City and at the White House for President and Mrs. Roosevelt.

1939 – Lincoln Memorial Concert. Receives NAACP's Spingarn Medal, presented by Eleanor Roosevelt.

1943 – Age 46. Marries Orpheus Fisher and lives in Danbury, Connecticut, on property they call Marianna Farm.

1955 – Debuts with the Metropolitan Opera in Un Ballo in Maschera, singing the role of Ulrica.

1958 – Appointed as United Nations alternate delegate to the Trusteeship Council.

1963 – Age 66. Performs at the March on Washington for Jobs and Freedom. Receives the Presidential Medal of Freedom two weeks after the death of President Kennedy.

1964 – Marian's mother, Anna Anderson, dies at age 89. Farewell American Tour begins at Constitution Hall.

1965 – Age 68. Easter Sunday. Last concert of the Farewell Tour at Carnegie Hall.

1977 – Age 80. Receives the United Nations Peace Prize.

1984 – Receives first Eleanor Roosevelt Human Rights Award.

1993 – Dies in Portland, Oregon, at age 96.

1997 – Centennial Tributes to Marian Anderson at Carnegie Hall and Union Baptist Church.

Selected Discography

The following recordings (available on compact disc) give a sampling of Marian Anderson's repertoire. Her aria from Verdi's *Un Ballo in Maschera* can be heard on *Bach. Brahms. Schubert*. With the exception of "Dear to the Heart of the Shepard" and "America" (which are not available on compact disc), all of the other song lyrics in this book can be heard on *Spirituals*.

— Marian Anderson, *Bach. Brahams. Schubert.*, BMG Music, New York, NY (1989).

— Marian Anderson, *Rare and Unpublished Recordings*, 1936–1952, VAI Audio, Pleasantville, NY (1998).

— Marian Anderson, *Schubert and Schumann Lieder*, BMG Entertainment, New York, NY (2000).

— Marian Anderson, *Spirituals*, BMG Entertainment, New York, NY (1999).

Dedicated to the memory of Richard Selznick

whose recollections inspired this book.

Text copyright © 2002 by . . . . Pam Muñoz Ryan

Illustrations copyright © 2002 by . . . . Brian Selznick

LIBRARY OF CONGRESS CATALOGING-IN-PUBLICATION DATA

Ryan, Pam Muñoz.

When Marian sang / written by Pam Muñoz Ryan; illustrated by Brian Selznick.—1st ed.   p. cm.

Summary: An introduction to the life of Marian Anderson, extraordinary singer and the first African American to perform with the Metropolitan Opera, whose life and career encouraged social change.

ISBN 0-439-26967-9

1. Anderson, Marian, 1897–1993—Juvenile literature. 2. Contraltos—United States—Biography—Juvenile literature. 3. African-American singers—Biography—Juvenile literature. [1. Anderson, Marian, 1897–1993. 2. Singers. 3. African Americans—Biography. 4. Women—Biography.] I. Selznick, Brian, ill. II. Title.   ML3930.A5 R93 2002   782.1'092—dc21   [B]   2001049508

10 9 8 7 6 5 4 3 2   02 03 04 05 06

Printed in . . . . Malaysia 46

First edition . . . . October 2002

The display type was set in . . . . Coronet Bold

The text type was set in . . . . 13-point Times Europa

The artwork was rendered in . . . . Liquitex Acrylics

Book design by . . . . Brian Selznick and David Saylor